Musings UNDER A Buckboard

a third compilation of poems

BY Rick Taylor

Copyright © 2019 by Rick Taylor

All rights reserved. No part of this book may be reproduced in any form or by any electronic or mechanical means including photocopying, recording and information storage and retrieval systems—except in the case of brief quotations imbedded in critical articles or reviews—without the permission in writing from the author.

Cover & Book Design: Scribe Freelance
www.scribefreelance.com

Published by:

CEZNO PRESS

ISBN: 978-0-578-53643-9

Printed in the United States of America

Contents

Musings Under a Buckboard 6
Stab Wounds 8
Keep the Engine Running 10
It Should Have Been Me 11
After the Fall 13
Bright Youth 15
Perspective Makes a Big Difference 16
Expanding Humanity 17
It Keeps on Ticking 19
Act Like a Bug 20
The Big Bang 21
The Meaning of Life 22
Devil-Dog 23
What's the Use? 24
Intersect 25
Burning with Joy 26
Zzzzzzzz 27
The Good Wife 28
Fetterman 29
Rousseau 31
Where Do Dead Birds Go? 32
The Urge to Purge 33
What is Intercourse? 34
A Real Brain 35
Daisy Fellowes 36
Daisy Fellowes (Part Two) 37
A Perfect Hawk 39
Black Bear 41

You Don't Look Seventy-Seven...43

Explosive Moments..44

Sabotage 45

Tilted Totem 46

Screams Prove the Bystander Effect..47

Shabby Intolerance..49

NMAAHC*..51

NMAAHC (Part Two)..53

Hush Money 55

Cannonball Run...56

A Woman of Style..58

Hawking Reaction 59

Who Needs Enemies? 61

Setup 63

Vapors Tossed 66

Vapors Tossed (Part Two)...68

To My Therapist...71

The Tower 73

Plucked..75

Wistful Thinking..76

Hacksaw Ridge...78

Aversion to Subversion 79

A Marble Index (Part Two)...81

My Favorite Poem..82

My Favorite Poem (Part Two) 85

Missed Opportunity...87

Often Bugged..89

Oscar Reborn..90

No Flashback 92

A Near-Death Experience *94*
Prelate Under Glass *96*
A Father She Can Trust *97*
Black Water *98*
Toppled Egos *99*
Memorable Neighbors *101*
Coco *103*
Reparations *105*
Acknowledgements *108*
About the Author *109*

Musings Under a Buckboard

Years ago, the shade available here
beneath this old buckboard
brought relief to my scorched frame.
Farm work was never ending in those days
and this secret place on the hill
brought welcome deliverance
from the sun's persistent rays.

I've come back
to restudy the breathtaking view,
a patchwork of multi-colored plots
unchanged to this day—
green, yellow, brown, and grey—
slanted downward toward a river
some distance away.
The stone cottage and church spire
also have something significant to say.

Back then, home-schooling seemed, at first,
to be a good way of dodging work,
but my mother's perfect logic and agreeable style
soon captured my interest, created a thirst.
At Kenyon, I couldn't get enough of Wordsworth,
Keats, Shelly, Coleridge, Byron, Arnold and the rest.
Superbly fortified by my mother's teaching,
I was able to ace almost every test.

Now the farm and both parents are gone,
and I've crawled back into my nest to brood.
Like Wordsworth, I've returned to a scene

that once produced *a serene and happy mood*.
However, the poet's thoughts and mine diverge
when in "Tintern Abbey"
Wordsworth describes *nature*
as the force that causes
all the world's beautiful parts to merge.
Mother always insisted that Christ alone
was the source of all creation,
and of all the beauty we could see.
It's sad that Mother wasn't available
to homeschool Wordsworth
with the thoughts she gave to me.

Stab Wounds

They called you Chuck,
a salesman with Valentino hair
that shined like wet coal.
You were a loving father full of care
whose kindness emerged from your very soul,
a father who did all the fatherly things
until two of your uncovered wires
happened to touch
a rare event, unexpected and dark,
unforgettable for anyone close enough
to witness the spark.

Rufus was known for leaving his unsavory packages
around the house if he wasn't let out at night.
Planning to be out late, you reminded me
to attend to him before I put out my light.
Of course, I forgot, but Rufus did not.
You had every right to be mad,
but my present thinking years later
is that you went too far.
YOU'RE LAZY AND SELF CENTERED.
YOU ONLY THINK OF YOURSELF.
WHEN WILL YOU EVER BE RESPONSIBLE?
This was said on top of your regular harangue.
It was much too much.
In your defense, you couldn't have known then
of my abnormal sensitivity
or of my battered body's proclivity
to leave flesh wounds untouched.

Mother gained excessive weight as a child.
Any teasing from other children created consternation
that her parents recognized as being far from mild.
When her brother joined in, it was much too much.
She balked at going to his funeral
and ignored any attempts by his family to keep in touch.
If my sister Jodi ever experienced similar taunting,
negative emotions on my mother's part
would inevitably erupt.
You adored my mother and catered to her whims.
On this sole issue, the distance between your bare wires
remained excessively thin.

How it happened I don't remember.
Jodi said something to me, and I said something back.
Unfortunately, I chose words in the forbidden area,
and soon I was under attack.
Your car took the corner on two wheels
and slammed to a stop at the place where I was standing.
Once again, your words were over the top
and at a volume that let the neighbors know
you could be very demanding.
YOU'RE LAZY AND SELF CENTERED.
YOU ONLY THINK OF YOURSELF.
HOW COULD YOU RIDICULE YOUR SISTER LIKE THAT?
YOU KNOW SHE GOES CRAZY WHEN ACCUSED OF BEING FAT.
I can't say your words didn't make me flinch.
They fashioned a picture of me
that has been with me ever since.

Keep the Engine Running

Nothing cuts like an unexpected obituary.
The name hits me between the eyes.
Adorable Susie never struck me
as the type of person who dies.
She was a blond-haired beauty
seven years my junior.
According to the obit,
she passed gallantly
with her family gathered round.

As if that's worth a fig.
If the Mormon Tabernacle Choir
gathered round me
singing hymns galore
I'd excuse myself, put on my slippers
and head for the bedroom door.
There's no sugar-coating Death.
Don't try to get comfortable.
Don't try to stall.
Just try to be somewhere else
when the Grim Reaper comes to call.

It Should Have Been Me

A carload of frolicking students
was traveling homeward from Yale.
Your brother was among them.
No one dreamed the brakes would fail.
One turn too many at too high a speed`
and the car ended up overturned in a field
after crashing through a stop sign
the driver couldn't heed.

You were young and naïve.
At first, the term *quadriplegic*
meant nothing to you,
but soon awareness of your brother's fate
gave you reason to grieve.
Stretched out on a raised bed,
he relied on a mirror tilted backwards
to communicate (when he was able).

He was all the things you weren't—
student body president, Phi Beta Kappa,
captain of two sports, a man women sought,
with a raging potential for greatness,
all of which ended in that isolated lot.
Too soon his condition caused him to die.
You stood at his gravesite
with smothered feelings, unable to cry.

After you married, from time to time
your wife would call my father
to say that you were drunk, raving madly,

and overcome by self-hate.
You were convinced that you should accept the blame
for your brother's dismal fate.
In your mind, you were worthless,
someone the world had learned to berate.
Dad's regular antidote
was a cold shower followed by lots of coffee.
Your refrain was the same every time you broke free.
You've got to understand. It should have been me.

After the Fall

Adam was away.
Eve was at home in the backyard,
reclining on a chaise.
Out of a hole in the ground
came the serpent
that Eve hadn't seen in many days.
Eve, I wonder if you remember me?
At first, she froze:
but in short order
she once again became composed:
How could I forget you? she said.
*You prompted the disobedience
that caused all our woes.*
The serpent responded:
There are a few things you ought to know.
He paused, then went on.
*Most important, you were set up, my Dear.
It was part of God's plan to bring evil into the world.
The Fallen Angels that mankind came to fear
were part of it.
As you probably know, nothing falls
outside of God's ambit.
The same is true regarding
your reaction to the famous tree.
Have you ever seen how most children perform
when you place them unsupervised
in a room full of candy that is plentiful and free?
At the end of the day
no matter how much you exhort them,
most of the candy will be eaten away.*

At first, Eve didn't know what to say.
Then, she pulled herself together
and answered in full voice.
Are you telling me that God
treated us like children knowing exactly
what we would do,
that I was a mere pawn?
The snake shot back,
Right on.
Remembering how beautiful Eden was,
Eve responded with a sheepish grin:
Considering that the fall was pre-planned,
is there any chance we can get back in?

Bright Youth

Bright youth.
How ephemeral can you get?
One moment I'm enthralled
by your silly games.
In the next
I'm tottering in place
struggling to remember names.

Perspective Makes a Big Difference

By early spring each leaf becomes determined
to be part of nature's Big Show.
Each is unaware, however,
that there are certain things
they aren't entitled to know.
Victims of nature's guile,
they redden with humiliation
when they finally learn
that soon they'll be part of a compost pile.
Had we but known the true facts, they say,
we'd have stayed green
and held on.
But each season comes anew
with a new crop of leaves
that have no clue
what will happen
when nature follows a course
that subverts and deceives.

Expanding Humanity

We must expand our humanity.
Boris, the leader of our Bible Study Group,
is inclined to make such pronouncements.
For a moment or two, silence prevails
and then the fusillade begins.
Amy is the first to haul up her sails.
Boris, what are you telling us?
Of course, we should expand our humanity.
And, yes, we should do it right now.
The question is **how**.
Boris clears his throat,
then answers in a loud voice.
Well, what do **you** *think, Amy?*
It's Boris's regular choice
to answer a question with a question.
Supposedly, it's a tactic to make us think.
I, for one, often fantasize about ringing his neck,
and right now, I'm on the brink.
Amy responds.
I'd look for a Webster definition
which usually is something meaningless
like "the quality of being human or humane."
Boris says that Amy's definition is perfect
which gives me another enormous pain.
He damn well knows
that her definition tells us nothing,
like a windsock hanging limp in the rain.
I'm known for liking people, and yet,
any time Boris enters the room, I begin to see red.
He looks like a character out of a Dickens novel,

except that Boris is not as wily or clever
as those about whom I've read.
Poor, dumb, boring, bald Boris,
a pariah he will always be.
His worst move was to steal
the head position of our study group,
a slot that should have gone to me.

It Keeps on Ticking

Twenty years, give or take.
That's far more than you can expect
with most appliances.
Even furnaces have been known to go
(usually in the dead of winter
when there's ten feet of snow).
By comparison, I refer to my own personal machinery.
How durable my circulatory system
has turned out to be.
For an average lifetime
the heart beats 3 billion score
and for me at age seventy-plus,
I'm hopeful it's prepared to beat
3 billion times more.
Still, I'm thankful
that mine has been beating
well beyond the average span.
To me it's an example of God's glory
and God's plan.
Each one of us is living proof
of the miracle known as *Man*.

Act Like a Bug

Have you ever noticed
that a tiny bug
fears for its life.
When I appear,
it scurries at full speed
for the underside of the washtub.
The brain of such an insect
can't be bigger than a speck.
Yet, the bug runs with the speed of Zeus
in an all-out effort to save its neck
(assuming it has a neck).
By contrast, you were a brilliant woman with
a brain much larger than that of a bug,
but you were prompted when angered or upset
to apply a strategy that was most unnerving.
Instead of trying to preserve your life,
as even the smallest bug would do,
you opened the car door
and attempted to jump through.
I always succeeded in pulling you back,
but when you were safe inside, I often thought
that it might make sense to let you succeed.
In the end, however, I always concluded
that anything was better
than watching you bleed.

The Big Bang

Your email stuns me—
It's over for me, you write.
I'm not willing to pursue this relationship any longer.
Take good care,
this after eight months of intense feeling.
Flowers and phone messages bring no response.
Your reaction sends me reeling.
Once well-placed in the universe
I now sense that I'm standing
one step too close to a black hole
that will stretch me beyond feeling.

The Meaning of Life

Pegasus
douses the mare's hindquarters
with a mushroom-shaped
ejaculation
even before Oppenheimer's
goggles began to jiggle,
causing Madame X
to grab her crotch
and giggle.

Devil-Dog

When our passion is drained,
you emerge from our love-soaked bed
with verbal blades flashing.
You have become a devil-dog
whose claws with one swipe
can cut off my head.
Passion and alcohol, always paired,
lull me into thinking
that this time the beast won't emerge.
In the end, however,
I discover that the devil-dog
will be my persistent adversary,
my ever-present scourge
so long as alcohol
remains an evil practice we can't purge.

What's the Use?

There's no point in criticizing Dr. Seuss,
I mean,
what's the use?
First and foremost, Dr. Seuss is dead.
Secondly, most of his young fans remain smitten
by the harvest of Seuss books they've read.
They're so enchanted, in fact, that they'll eat
green eggs and ham,
or green eggs alone
or ham alone (without the bone).
Still, I must say it.
I can no longer delay it:
Dr. Seuss didn't want to have kids around.
You have the kids
and I'll entertain them,
he once said.
Imagine that!
None of the little people
who loved the Cat in the Hat
were ever found on his living room rug
or in the upstairs hall
or in the attic,
if you can believe that at all.
Quite honestly, when I learned
of his aversion to having children,
any kind of kid—
tall, short, skinny or fat—
for me, the fizz
went out of the Cat in the Hat.

Intersect

Lincoln in his famous dream
asked a crucial question of a soldier
standing in place—
Who is dead in the White House?
With a look of despondency on his face
the soldier answered—
It's the President. He been killed by an assassin.

Lincoln's dream provided an intersect
between a dreamworld
and the location of his initial resting place.
On some level, he was being told
he would soon be displaced.
A snake at times can see its tail.
Likewise, fate sometimes coils backward
in a way that gives us an opportunity to learn
what the future will entail.
Reluctantly, Lincoln learned the score—
extended fame and immortality come after death,
not before.

Burning with Joy

I'm burning with joy,
bursting with feelings I cannot stop.
Outside my window
I see snow drifted up like Cool Whip
with tiny footprints evident in various tracks
visible on top.
It's a winter scene that God has blessed,
ready for framing by Currier and Ives.

A week later, that same snow covering
is blasted by the afternoon sun
which has jack-hammered what is left.
It is an important moment
that proclaims to one and all
that winter is on the run.

I'm buoyed up by the idea of spring,
but it seems to me it should be heralded
by something more significant than melting snow.
Instead, when it comes to a head,
there should be angelic voices singing,
blasting trumpets trumpeting
and pounding drums drumming
unless we are all dead.

Zzzzzzz

Because of my advancing years,
it's getting tougher
and tougher to arise.
Each morning
I add another few seconds
to any previous prize.
If this keeps up,
when I'm ninety-four
I'll be sleeping all month
and hoping for more.

The Good Wife

The first word is *strong*
then comes *attractive* and *bright*
followed by *loyal* and *organized*.
Best of all, Shannon has a big heart
full of love that overflows
with a special kind of affection
for everyone she knows.
Her organizational skills come to the fore
when she plans a vacation,
pays the bills,
or determines what we can afford.
Similarities between us are easily found.
She's a widow and I'm a widower
and Pittsburgh is the city
where both of us were found.
Each of us has three children
and five grandchildren.
Best of all, she has never tried to stand between
me and my rhyme,
even though I often lose myself on my PC
for hours at a time.
There are differences as well,
especially in politics.
She is a moderate
and I'm a conservative.
However, when the family's left wing begins its attack,
Shannon is always there to cover my back.
Even a short study makes it easy to see
that the biggest test for this little pixie
is putting up with me.

Fetterman

Br'er Rabbit begged his tormentors
to avoid tossing him into the briar patch,
which, of course, was exactly what they did.
They didn't realize that the briar patch
was a safe place for him,
a haven where he often hid.
It's too bad this children's story
didn't give Fetterman a clue
about what to do when Crazy Horse
and a few braves enticed him to do
what they wanted him to do.
Don't go over the ridge,
Fetterman's Commander had said.
If you do, you're likely to end up dead.
But Captain Fetterman
had eighty troopers at his command
and had served with distinction in the Civil War.
No bloody Indian is going to call my hand,
he thought, as he went out the door.

As he passed through the fort's front gate,
his Commander said yet again,
Don't go over the ridge. It may be a trap.
But the Indians on the hill were mooning him
and shouting insults.
Fetterman never looked back.
He charged the hill at full gallop
and chased the rowdy Indians over the ridge
where a huge force of hostiles was waiting to attack.
Eighty troopers were lost under Fetterman's command.

Unlike Custer, this had not been a noble stand.
Fetterman is a prime example
of what happens when hubris gets out of hand.
He'll go down in history as a fool.
But that won't help the men who followed him.
They suffered in a briar patch
that turned out to be extremely cruel.

Rousseau

Rousseau has said that the human body begins to die
from the moment of its birth.
Today a mirror grabbed me as I passed by
showing no mercy and no mirth.
Your forehead is rutted, the mirror said,
your eyes are bagged,
your neck has sagged, your hair is grey.

Now in my seventies and not extremely brave,
I'm certain Rousseau would say,
You have one foot in the grave.
I never saw it coming.
It crept over me like a glove.
Decrepit as I am,
I'm lucky I have someone to love.
When the lid comes down,
I'm sure that Shannon will be there.
But because of my failure to interact with others
as I favor my experiments in verse,
she may have to fill the pews
with mannikins or even homeless vagrants,
which, of course would be ten times worse.
It's not just my reclusive tendencies
that will cause the sanctuary to be bare.
A dead conservative in Shepherdstown
is a phenomenon that is very threatening
and extremely rare.

Where Do Dead Birds Go?

How many dead birds do we see?
If your experience has been akin to mine,
the absence of bird body parts is an enigma
that has remained a mystery to me.
The Bible speaks favorably of birds
and the conclusion I draw from this assessment
is something I never expected.
The reason we don't find bird corpses,
is because, when they die, they've resurrected.

The Urge to Purge

Father in Heaven,
our Republic stands,
but for how long?
Decay is impossible to curtail,
and evil is ever surging.
In order to slow the raging pace of both,
shouldn't you resort to serious purging?
The Lord's response
was a surprise to me.
I don't need to take action.
Don't you see?
Mankind will carry out
its own purging without any urging from me.

What is Intercourse?

Dad, what's intercourse?
Oh, to be back to those innocent days
when my son would ask me questions like that.
I don't remember the answer I gave,
but it was enough to hold him,
'til his mother got back.

A Real Brain

You lived in our neighborhood,
the son of a scientist, a real brain.
How I envied you
as I struggled with numbers
and grades that gave my parents
continuing pain.
I hung onto every word you said.
I must ask, though,
what good will your brainpower be,
now that you are dead?

Daisy Fellowes

Author, poet, editor,
and great granddaughter
to a sewing machine magnate.
Rich beyond compare.
Twentieth century seductress extraordinaire.
Described as the most wicked woman in High Society.
A goddess of excess laid bare.
Two yachts on hand fully staffed.
Outfits to make people stare
(but no one dared laugh.)
Dripping in jewelry, each precious item a different size.
Habitué of Paris, London, Monte Carlo.
A net worth that continued to rise.
A lover of priceless antiques.
A darling of courtiers, jewelers,
and owners of exclusive boutiques.
A color (shocking pink) designed especially for her.
She lived on grouse, cocaine,
and any available spouse.
On the tragic side,
Daisy had a mother who killed herself
when Daisy was four.
At the age of seventy-two during a reclusion
(ten years in which she chose to hide)
Daisy Fellowes, alone in her hotel room
lay down on her single bed and died.

Daisy Fellowes (Part Two)

My mother (of humble origin)
speculated about the wealthy a lot:
Are they truly happy? She often asked.
I think not.
I always suspected that jealousy
motivated mother's slanted insight.
That is until I read about Daisy
and her family after which
I concluded that my mother
may have been right.
Even with all the great wealth,
Daisy's mother, Isabelle-Blanche Singer,
at the tender age of 27 took her own life.
Several times Daisy tried unsuccessfully
to follow her mother's lead
as a reaction to what she saw
as life's unending strife.
When I described these things to mother
her reaction was quite predictable:
You see, you see.
You should listen to me.
I didn't tell mother about the rest.
The worst chapter in Daisy's life
occurred toward the end of the war
when Daisy suffered deep remorse
because Jacqueline, her daughter in Paris,
showed she had taken the wrong course.
Jacqueline was found to be a collaborator
and Jacqueline's husband, Alfred Kraus,
was charged with being a spy

who had informed on members of the Resistance
all of whom would later die.
Sometime after Jacqueline's divorce from Kraus,
her ex-husband disappeared quite suddenly
in London away from his house
when he was pulled into a passing car.
Some say he was assassinated at Churchill's insistence
as retribution for conduct disloyal and bizarre
that was so disastrous
to the Resistance during the war.
I didn't tell mother about Daisy's post-war disgrace
because at the time I read of it
mother had already proven her case.

A Perfect Hawk

I saw today a perfect hawk
perched in our tree
with his full attention
directed at me.
He sat unfluffed
as though ready to talk
as I studied him from my car.
He elected to stay
even when
I opened the window
to hear what he had to say.
Silence prevailed
as he stared back.
Did he come as an omen,
or to pursue an attack?
Or did he come to satisfy
some ritual or fad?
If an omen, was it good
or was it bad?
When no words were said,
he pushed out his buff-colored chest
as if to show his anger
at my failing to pass
his hawkish test.
When he spread his wings
as a preamble to flying away,
I could see two white stripes
on the underside of each black wing.
In one fell swoop
he fled the scene,

(flew the coop)
leaving me to cogitate
on what his presence might mean.

Black Bear

As if one omen isn't enough,
Shannon soon after has a chilling nightmare
that provides yet another warning
that times could soon be tough.
After the dream,
she chooses her words carefully.

I notice movement off to my right.
Then I see that it's a black bear
of enormous size
Avoid eye contact! I say.
Cover your head!
As usual, you ignore my advice
and I conclude that
you'll soon be dead.
The bear picks a spot
directly in front of you
where he rises to his full height,
before lunging for your head
presumably to take a bite.
And then I wake up.
It's the middle of the night.

Whoa! I say in response.

Yesterday I witnessed
the close presence of a perched hawk
that gave the impression
he had stopped by to talk.
When the bird took flight,

the underside of his wings
displayed a color black as night.
On top of that,
you describe your bear
as being coal-black,
which symbolizes death, of course.
Are the bear and the hawk
part of a spiritual force
telling me I'll soon be feeling
the hot breath of death's pale horse?

Not one to take chances or to raise a fuss
the next day I quietly drive off to Hagerstown
to visit *Shrouds-Are-Us.*

You Don't Look Seventy-Seven

You don't look seventy-seven.
At coffee-hour at church,
a fellow parishioner says this to me.
On the way home,
I remember that father died at eighty-two
and mother at seventy-four.
Under that scenario, I should already be dead
or lucky to live five years more.
In any case, I'm alerted to the fact
that the black horse of death
might soon be approaching.
At home that same day, I pray
that my sins be forgiven,
an act of contrition
made necessary by unacceptable conduct
in prior years caused by a bipolar condition.
After the correct prognosis is given,
I discover with the help of correct medication
a world that often seems sublime,
a higher plane where life takes on a new façade
that is not only new but fresh.
It is a transformation that comes just in time.
At that moment, I'm close enough to hell
to smell the burning flesh.

Explosive Moments

When I'm asked, *how bad was it
in the meatgrinder?*
I avoid providing the details they seek.
Instead, because of my concern for privacy
I answer with tongue-in-cheek.
I start with the worst.

*Shaking a bottle of V-8 when the top is loose.
Juice sprayed all over kitchen cabinets
makes me feel like a ruptured moose.*

*Discovering while eating a hard-boiled egg
that a shell fragment is still in place.
To me it's like getting a root canal,
but on the issue of pain, I'm a special case.*

*Drinking from an open can of beer
only to discover
a cigarette butt floating inside.*

By then, the inquirer usually has decried
that my answers, though innocent when supplied,
can never be classed as bona fide.

Sabotage

When I'm in my negative mode
the world is suddenly draped in black crepe.
It's usually a throwback to my bipolar days
when my emotions regularly searched for a way to escape.
My doctor now assures me
that it's just a depressive phase
that will go away quickly *as I begin to age.*
Begin to age?
Why does my doctor grin?
I expect that in my case he knows,
that my aging process isn't *coming,*
it's been.

Tilted Totem

At the Totem Pole Playhouse,
we listened to Hank Williams and Patsy Kline.
I was anxious to see what they both looked like
after Hank's overdose and Patsy's crash.
Despite these shortcomings,
their act was a smash.

Screams Prove the Bystander Effect

I heard the screams and crying,
the kind an infant might make,
not when it's hungry,
but when it's dying,
the kind of caterwaul
that raises the hairs
on your arms and back.
I once heard baby rabbits
screaming like that
in the dead of night,
when a fox decided to attack.
By contrast, the current screams
come in broad daylight
from a murder-scene up high.
A hawk is extracting baby squirrels
from a nest in a nearby tree.
Nature's course
should be open and free
with no interference coming from me.

Poppycock.

I could have screamed at the hawk
to send it away,
but I didn't.
I had nothing to say.
Afterward, I thought of Kitty Genovese
in New York City
and of the many unfortunate Jewish families
in Berlin and elsewhere at the time of war.

Even though mayhem was occurring
out in the street and up the hall,
no one offered any assistance to the victims,
no assistance at all.
Of course, baby squirrels aren't as valuable
as we are, as should be apparent.

Poppycock.

When any baby squirrel is murdered
 in broad daylight,
the effect is always colossal.
It is shattering to any squirrel family.
Just ask either parent.

Shabby Intolerance

Before dawn, unable to sleep.
I sit in my office-chair
studying a nearby street.
Illuminated by streetlight,
a scraggy specimen ambles by
with long, thin legs,
large pointed ears, an extended snout,
and large yellow teeth
displayed in an open mouth
that shows a long tongue hanging out.
A fox? No, too big.
A coyote? Perhaps.
A dog? It wasn't a dog.
On that you can depend.
No dog's coat ever looked like that one—
frizzy, wispy, with occasional dark patches,
like a hobo bent on proving
by his slouching gait
and mottled coat
that he has no money to spend.
I see this animal several times more.
Brazened as he is, and bright,
he's equally comfortable
coming in the morning or at night.
His gusto earns my respect,
but the members of the Unit Owner's Association
show a different side.
They aren't willing to negotiate.
They want the poor animal's hide.
An unfamiliar animal is something

the group cannot abide.
A short time later,
my mysterious friend
disappears without a trace.
Admittedly, he was ugly.
It was a trait I tried to erase.
Later, I have words for him
that I wanted to give him
face to face.
Forgive me,
for failing to come to your aid.
As a conservative in a liberal town,
I know the impact that intolerance
can make.
In your case, the villagers were out for blood,
(or so it would seem).
Don't you see?
The strategy they trump up for you
is the same, without the blood (so far),
that they trump up for me.
If in 2020 Trump wins the fight,
I'll have to buy a bullet-proof vest
and stop going out at night.

NMAAHC*

The African American Museum in D.C.
is undoubtedly the best museum I'll ever see.
It reminds me of a Step Pyramid constructed in a much earlier day
and the exterior is golden in color like the Arc of the Covenant
that held so many enemies at bay.
The interior dazzles me even more,
with perfect displays
showing what slavery victims had to endure.
The brochure reports
a quarter-billion-dollar building cost
split between willing donors
and a generous government.
Later, at a party, I ask a question
of a woman of color
who is young and beautifully dressed.
By building this fantastic structure
hasn't the nation passed
any applicable anti-racist test?
She responds.
Keep in mind, the victims of slavery
were stolen from their African homes,
crammed into waiting ships,
chained to fellow victims who would probably die,
and choked by a pervading stench during passage
that would make any sane man cry.
And that may have been the best part
compared to what lay ahead on shore
when the women were systematically raped,
and both men and women were forced
to work twelve hour shifts or more.

I respond.
Yes, but didn't a lot of soldiers
become casualties of war
while fighting to end slavery
and the brutal prejudice
the world had come to abhor?

Her response is quick.
Half fought to keep us chained.
Retribution for the sin of slavery
meant that oceans of blood had to be spilled.
That is why the war was so long maintained
and why so many graves were filled.

I respond.
I agree with what you're saying.
I think you've given the correct point of view.
No shrine or magnificent structure
or dollar amount could ever attune
for the deadly practice
that dragged our nation into war.

*National Museum of African American History and Culture

NMAAHC (Part Two)

A week later I spot the same woman
in the Sweet Shop on German Street
where residents of Shepherdstown often go.
She is sitting alone
and asks me to join her
for a coffee and a scone.
She begins.
I wanted to add some comments
to our conversation the other night.
Yes, slavery ended, but bigotry and prejudice
continued to hold on tight.
For a time, lynching wasn't illegal,
and the KKK resorted to that practice a lot.
When reconstruction ended,
segregation came close behind.
Separate but equal was a continuing disgrace
along with seats on buses that were assigned
to all members of our race.
Even if oceans of blood were spilled to end slavery,
that won't compensate my people
for what has happened since?

I respond.
Yes, but in recent years
the pendulum has swung back to its proper place.
Think of the changes that have occurred.
Today examples of segregation are very rare,
and you don't often hear the n-word.
shouted into another person's face
Your voting rights are now protected

*and in many cases
your own candidates have received a winning score.
It's all happened in good time.
Have patience and stay tuned for more.*

She responds.
*If that is what you believe
in the face of all our trouble,
who am I to prick your bubble?*

We smile at each other in silence
as if there's nothing more to say.
I stand up to take my leave
and slowly walk away.

Hush Money

I overhear two ladies talking in a coffee house:
First: *Did you hear?*
Second: *Hear what, my dear?*
First: *The President has proven himself to be a complete louse.*
Second: *How so?*
First: *He signed and sent a check for hush money while he was President, right out of the White House.*
Second: *That's something I didn't know?*
First: *Where have you been? Don't you read the newspapers? The payment was intended to keep a woman quiet about an affair.*
Second: *Tell me more.*
First: *The tryst occurred fifteen years ago with a porn star with long blond hair.*
Second: *If that's true, isn't it time for impeachment proceedings to begin?*
At that point, a group of teenagers walk in. I want to inject some comments but can't because of the din. I want to say that Clinton's tryst took place in the White House whereas Trump's occurred several years before he got there, and that Clinton has left us with an image of a president's spilled seed on an intern's blue dress. If Clinton got off scot free, should Trump expect any less?

Cannonball Run

How can I be anything but miffed?
I'm having a perfectly good day
when suddenly there comes a shift
when a memory comes hurtling into my consciousness
like a cannonball traveling at warp speed.
In a flash, in my mind's eye,
I see my deceased wife and me
in great need
in an unfamiliar part of town,
returning home from a party
whose hosts encouraged us
to stay too long and drink too much.
We realize that the drive to our home
on the other side of town will be daunting.
My bad driving, particularly my excessive speed,
produces wrong turns on unfamiliar streets
and inspires my wife's incessant taunting.
The road ends with a barrier unseen, and a hard smash
preceded by slamming brakes and sliding ice.
Although your upper torso hits the dash,
no blood is spilled, and the car is undamaged
in what appears to be a minor crash.

Later, in the silence of my living room
I hear an anger-filled voice from the other side:
You didn't see what that mishap would do to me.
You laughed it off.
At the time, I was cancer-free.
The impact, seemingly minor,
awakened in me every dormant cancer cell.

The ovarian tumor came soon after,
a scourge that produced a living hell.
I respond.
I don't accept your scheme
to create consternation and woe.
It was a minor event that happened in Mount Lebanon
a long time ago.
I always assumed that the afterlife, where you are now,
would be a place abounding in love and peace,
and here you are peddling a unique brand of guilt
intended to disrupt any sense of release.

She responds.
If you're implying that I'm not in a divine space,
your logic is poor.
I've been given the run of the place by Saint Peter.
(who could ever ask for more?).
He insists that I make good use of my time up here.
In his view, that should include time spent
causing disruption below.
Widowers are the best targets, he says.
It gives the deceased wife a chance to even the score.
Plus, we're doing the husband a favor.
Without guilt trips like this one,
your life on earth would be a shattering bore.

A Woman of Style

I'm reading about Rita Lydig*
and other women of style from a prior age,
when, in an instant, an image of you
flashes into my memory.
I see you coming down a long corridor
at the Pittsburgh Golf Club
on your way to the grill where we are sitting.
You are dressed in a smashing outfit
with a colorful scarf around your neck
that is perfectly fitting.
Your clothes are part of it,
but the real impact comes from a marriage
of beauty, brilliance and pervading confidence
expressed in your self-assured carriage.
Rita Lydig was asked by Sarah Bernhardt
to demonstrate a proper walk.
Rita's directions [paraphrased] you already know.
Never on the heels, only the balls of the feet
and not too heavily even then,
lightly touching on the ground,
head held high with deep breaths applied,
feeling the spring of it on one's entire spine.
Imagine Sara Bernhardt, a famous actress, being so stupefied
by a woman whose walk had never graced a stage.
Rita, Sara said, had a quality—
which I have never found in anyone else—
of radiating artistic creativeness.
Speaking in a different age,
Sarah Bernhardt had chosen words
that applied to Rita
and to you.

*Tapert, Annette and Edkins, Diana. THE POWER OF STYLE.
Random House: New York. 1994. pp.15, 18.

Hawking Reaction

Stephen, your book*
I've just read
and I have got so many questions.
It's unfortunate you're dead.
You conclude there's no God,
and, as if that's not enough,
you also conclude *there's **probably** no
heaven or afterlife either* [my emphasis].
As a practicing Christian,
I find your conclusions to be a bit rough,
but I hesitate to criticize since you're not around
to call my bluff.

Oh, what the heck
I'm going to venture forth anyway,
even though I may be exposing my neck.
In describing the Big Bang,
you conclude that just before it happened
the universe got very, very small.
In fact, according to you,
it became *an infinitesimally small,
infinitesimally dense black hole,* and that's all.
Some might say that over the course of your career
you've been hung up by black holes,
so, it's not at all queer
that you'd speculate about yet another.
Even assuming you're correct,
can anyone tell us what might be on the other side?
(If so, that's something I'd really like to hear).
Additionally, so far, no scientist

has reduced the puzzle of *Dark Matter*
to a formula that would provide chapter and verse.
Nor has any scientist opened the door
that has been hiding details regarding
a Parallel Universe.
As often occurs with sex, your decision
to bring your views to fruition
has been a bit premature.
Don't you see?
At a time when (for many)
the existence of religion is on the brink,
you've removed crucial avenues of faith
that nurture humanity's soul, and you did it without a wink.
Worst of all, you used words like **probably**,
a word that gives your opinion a negative twist.
Hopefully, when you meet Saint Peter up above
you can insist
that you've given up your premature thinking
in favor of a mantra that is **LOVE**.

*Hawking, Stephen. BRIEF ANSWERS TO BIG QUESTIONS.
Bantam: New York. 2018.
p.38.

Who Needs Enemies?

Side by side
we hit used golf balls into the lake,
conferring after each shot.
Yours travel straight and far.
Mine do not.
You are brimming with bad advice.
Sway into the shot, you lie,
when you know full well
that a pivot using a corkscrew effect
would keep me satisfied.
Your mother invites me to visit all summer
at her cottage above the lake (Chautauqua)
and the rivalry between us is an unexpected twist
that turns out to be more than I can take.
Kristen is blond-haired and beautiful,
a girl I love intensely who from the start
promises a relationship of great bliss.
I have no idea you have your own designs
until one night under the stars
when you emerge from behind a hedge
at the very moment I'm moving in to give her a kiss.
A Texas boy with a drawl I know is fake,
you drive your dated white Jaguar from Texas
and park it to be near Kristen's cottage
which is down by the lake.
Allegedly, you park there to use her hose,
but your mother's cottage gives you similar access,
making your true motives in being there
something I can easily expose,
but I restrain myself for Kristin's sake

although it took everything in my power
to keep from pushing your Jaguar into the lake.

Setup

ME: *I think I'm on to something.*
BORIS: *Do tell?*
We are sitting with several others in a prayer group meeting after church. I intend to add a little excitement to a meeting that is always dull and long. Unfortunately, the Holy Spirit must have taken the afternoon off because my negative feelings about Boris are still in place and strong. I've described him in another poem, so I won't bother doing so here. In time, I've come to see that he's an obnoxious little bastard who feels that there's nothing better than taking shots at me, a tendency I've always found to be extremely queer.
ME: *Well, we've been talking about the crucifixion—*
BORIS: *—what brilliant insights do you want to share with us about that?*
ME: *I'm convinced it was all orchestrated.*
What do you say to that?
BORIS: *Orchestrated?*
ME: *Damn straight.*
BORIS: *Do tell. This should be great.*
ME: *Well, take Judas, for example. Jesus knew that Judas would be his betrayer.*
BORIS: *I think that's clear. To recognize that, you don't have to be a seer.*
ME: *How would you want to be that unlucky cluck? He had a brand on him from the start and the brand couldn't be chucked. He would always be flat out of luck.*
BORIS: *You don't mean an actual brand... like something you might find on a Trump supporter?*
ME: *Of course not. And watch what you say about Trump supporters being dumb.*
I say that because I happen to be one.

BORIS: *Oh, great. You support a man who knows how to lie.*
Because I'm on a mission, I let his comment slip by.
ME: *Judas is slated to do what he did and ends up hanging himself from a tree. You've got to feel sorry for him. Don't you see?*
BORIS: *I don't feel sorry for him. He was stealing from the common purse.*
ME: *And for that he should roast in hell and suffer an eternal curse? Particularly when he was set up in such a way as to leave him no way to shift into reverse.*
BORIS: *That's because he went from bad to worse.*
ME: *All right. Let's move in a different direction. When I say it was all orchestrated, I look to the Psalms for support. Psalm 22:1 reads as follows:*
"MY GOD, MY GOD, why hast thou forsaken me?"
The Psalms were written long before the crucifixion. Yet, these are the very words Jesus uses on the cross. In other words, that verse foretells what will happen later when things get hotter.
BORIS: *Your argument doesn't hold water.*
ME: *Why is that?*

It's all I can do to keep from jumping over the table to show with my fist that I'm not a fan. But I hold my temper because that would interfere with my plan. I'm setting him up just as Judas was set up and I must keep to the script as best I can.

BORIS: *Jesus was a scholar. He knew the Psalms backward and forward. He simply recited on the cross what he already had memorized. I think that's easy to see.*

What he is saying, of course, is that it would be easy to see for anyone but a stupid ass like me. I don't mind the slur because it reminds me that patience is to be the key.

ME: *Boris, you may be forgetting another verse, Psalm 22:18 which provides as follows:*

"They put my garments among them and cast lots upon my vesture."

John 19:23 also speaks of this;

"When the soldiers had crucified Jesus, they took his garments and divided them into four parts, one part for each soldier; also, his tunic. But the tunic was seamless, woven in one piece from top to bottom, so they said to one another, 'Let's not tear it, but cast lots for it to see whose it shall be.' This was to fulfill the scripture which says,

"They divided my garments
among them
and for my clothing they cast lots."

How do you account for that, Boris? Did the four soldiers also memorize their parts?

He could see that I had him. His cherubic face turned from red to white. His words wouldn't come. He couldn't say more. He lifted his pudgy little body out of his chair and headed for the door.

Vapors Tossed

An anthology* opened blindly
to reveal "I Am" by John Clare,
a poet who experienced extreme lows
causing regular attendance in lunatic asylums.
In the words he chooses, his agony clearly shows:

> I am [,] yet what I am none cares or knows:
>   My friends forsake me like a memory lost
> I am the self-consumer of my woes—
>   They rise and vanish in obvious host
> Like shadows in love's frenzied stifled throes—
> And yet I am, and live like vapors tossed
>
> Into the nothingness of scorn and noise
> Into the living sea of waking dreams
> Where there is neither sense of life [nor] joys
> But the vast shipwreck of my life's esteems…

Whereas I describe a *meatgrinder,*
Clare uses the word *shipwreck.*
As with me, it amounts to
a noose around one's neck,
but there is one aspect
that is even more compelling.
He suffers without medication.
Yet, even when the *shipwreck* of his life
tosses him into *the living sea,*
he longs for a paradise free of strife—

> There to abide with my Creator; God,

And sleep as I in childhood sweetly slept
Untroubling and untroubled where I lie,
The grass below—above the vaulted sky.

He mirrors my own quest for a spiritual connection
but Clare does it without the gift of Lithium,
thereby proving the desperation in his search for protection.

* Harmon, William, ed. THE TOP FIVE HUNDRED POEMS. New York: Columbia University Press, 1992. p. 528.

Vapors Tossed (Part Two)

CEZNO:* What the hell is that last poem about?
ME: It's not obvious to you? That really cuts.

We're in a booth at Betty's *after finishing breakfast. This is the place to go if you are in Shepherdstown, West Virginia, with a hankering for such things as eggs over easy with coffee, sausage and toast. It's the diner in this town that the breakfast crowd seems to like the most.*

CEZNO: The meaning of your poem sure isn't obvious to me...unless you're saying that Heaven is available only to people who are nuts.
ME: That's not it at all, although Clare's type of negative thinking often nests in people who are living very troubled lives.
CEZNO: What about the rest of us who are looking for meaning that survives?
ME: Many begin a spiritual walk by asking God to come into their lives. The truth is that He's already there, in our hearts. It's something we've already got.
 CEZNO: Next, you'll be telling me that God knocks on a door inside of us and we must decide whether to open it or not.
ME: What you just said is Biblical. You have stumbled onto a Biblical precept.
CEZNO: If it's a spiritual precept, I'm sure you'll tell me it was heaven-sent. Next, you'll tell me that your poem, the one you just read, describes a real-life event.
ME: It was a real-life event. I opened the anthology to Clare's poem without even knowing who he was. Considering what's in the poem, I'm convinced that my selection wasn't my own invention. If I seemed to imply that, it wasn't my intention.
CEZNO: Is this what some people call *divine intervention*? If I listen to you, I must conclude that God's invisible hand swooped down like a

hook and forced you to select that exact page in your poetry book.
ME: Sometimes it's very subtle, as in this case. Other times it's very pronounced, as with the three taps on my shoulder on the airport road that saved me from certain death. To me, the airport incident was divine intervention in its most telling form, and I'll insist upon that until my last breath.
CEZNO: I don't buy it. *You're specially blessed.* That's what you want to say.
ME: You can believe what you will, but I can tell you right now, I experience God's presence in my life every day.
CEZNO: That's hard to believe considering that God must also worry about such things as the universe and nuclear war. He has good excuses to stay away.
ME: I don't know how He does it. It's often done in a very subtle way. It might be that the intervention is accomplished with the help of an emissary…an angel, a deceased loved one or the Holy Spirit, but I can tell you one thing—I feel guided by a force that I hope is here to stay.
CEZNO: If you're hearing voices, there may be a funny farm waiting for you, or even a nest in a tree.
ME: Speaking of craziness, I can tell you that going through *the meatgrinder* did wonders for me. Before appropriate medication came, I was a poor specimen—self-centered, arrogant, and at times unable to concentrate, debilitated as I was by depression or extreme mania. I didn't like myself at all. It just wasn't right.
CEZNO: But then you saw the light.
ME: My trip through the rathole, though painful, also provided huge benefits because on the other side, I've been transformed, reborn, thanks to Lithium, into something even I can stand, but it didn't happen overnight.
CEZNO: *I understand*, the hangman said.
ME: I've also had a chance to study other victims of bipolar disease in several books I've read.
CEZNO: Go on.
ME: There were many suicides—Ernest Hemingway, Anne Sexton, Virginia Woolf, Sylvia Plath, Hart Crane, Randall Jarrell are just a few

of the ones who ended up dead.
CEZNO: The disease back then was a killer that no apparent treatment could quell.
ME: Marriages were torn apart as well. I think of Hemingway, Robert Lowell, T.S. Eliot, F. Scott Fitzgerald and Virginia Woolf, all of whom went through a living hell.
CEZNO: All were excellent writers as well. You might call bipolar disease a badge of honor. I'm sure you'd be willing to experience it all again, considering the enhanced writing talent that would be available at your bidding.
ME: You've got to be kidding.
CEZNO: I'm surprised at your reaction since we both know that Lithium will cover your flanks.
ME: Lithium or not I'd never go through the meatgrinder again. For making such a suggestion I can offer you no thanks.

At that point we got up from the table and moved toward the door.
"Hey, how about paying the check," *our waitress was calling.*
"Oh, sorry, I'll take care of it right away," *I said.*
I pretended that I intended to pay it all along, but if the truth be known, the intensity of the conversation had caused a definite numbness in my head.

*My imaginary friend (you're never too old). In fact, growing up, I was my neighbor's imaginary friend.

To My Therapist

Psychotherapy with you once a week
for eight long years
was an opportunity for you to discover
the overriding source of all my fears.
My life, a heap of smoldering ruin,
had put me on the brink.
With manic fires consuming me,
my brain was raging in a way
that made it impossible to think.
All this was combined with a flight of ideas,
a rapid flow of speech,
hyperactivity and dark moods.
Only one prognosis was possible to reach:
Bipolar Disease (also known as manic/depressive illness).
If you'd prescribed Lithium early on,
I'm convinced that at least part
of my early failings could have been detoured.
In many cases (as ultimately occurred with me)
when Lithium is applied
the patient's sanity is quickly restored.
However, if there's any link
between madness and creativity at all,
it follows that a prolonged period in the meatgrinder
might have been an appropriate call.
Inside the meatgrinder,
I was being pounded into a new person,
reborn in a way that helped me
to produce a body of work
that some say surpasses anything
I'd written before.

Still, I refuse to thank you
for the late prognosis.
Time in that monstrous place
served to cut me to the core.
Any prospect of prolonging it
is something to abhor.

The Tower

Canada was our summer place
years ago.
Several times
we travelled to Chateau Woodland
near Haliburton, Ontario
beside a lake
whose Indian name
I could never pronounce
with my childish voice,
let alone spell.
In the early years,
that rustic spot
was our inevitable choice.

A wooden tower
painted white
stood at the end
of the Inn's private dock,
seemingly quite high
(to pre-teenage eyes)
though years of memory
have reduced its size.
Davitt, an only child,
spawned by family friends,
was always there.
My same age,
Davitt, bereft of confidence
from over-coddling,
was unable to jump
from the tower's top-level.

No amount of teasing or cajoling
could sway him
even though my sister and I,
acting like otters,
made many a laughing leap.
into the lake's clear and frigid waters.

Later in life, Davitt
became a hopeless drunk,
an addiction that finally killed him,
thankfully with a speedy release
that ended Davitt's regular practice
of hide and cower.
I couldn't help but wonder
whether the slide into that wretched abyss
began with his refusal to jump off the tower.
If he'd jumped, would he have
stepped out of the ugly life he got?
Probably not.

Plucked

I hear the sputter of my engine as it dies.
My crashed spotter plane is caught in the trees.
When I regain consciousness,
I discover that my right eye
is the only eye that sees.
My wound has sprayed blood
over the cockpit on the window's inside.
I mustn't cry out.
Vietcong patrols are everywhere.
If an unrecognized sound alerts them,
they will be glad to take me out.

A year ago, I recoiled at the thought of war,
yet here I am,
jammed in with no place to go.
There's no getting out.
Lord, if this is the place where I'm destined to die,
here in Vietnam,
please help me to understand why.

Wistful Thinking

I know, you're an angry spouse
waiting for me up there.
You've been unfair to me, you'll say,
*in the way you describe my life.
A devoted husband
should be brimming over
with good things to say
about a departed wife.*
You'll then assure me
that because of my various poetic criticisms,
I've forgotten all the good things
about our extended married life.
In fairness, in those poems
I should have added
that the highlighted bad moments
were few and far between.
Still, I would never argue
that the later years of my life with you
were either soothing or serene.
You were gorgeous and brilliant
(bordering on genius) with perfect breasts
and splendid legs.
A good friend didn't hesitate to tell me
that he couldn't help but imagine the good sex
a perfect body like yours would entertain.
You gave me three wonderful children
while living with me through my meatgrinder days.
In the early years, good times far exceeded the bad.
Our drinking gradually increased, however,
until the cocktail hour became
much more than just a momentary fad.

As my Southern Comfort Manhattans
and your Martinis became serious fare,
it came to the point where one drink
could put us over the brink,
but we could never decide
whether it was the fifth or sixth
that produced an inability to think.
It was then that the hot lava
in your emotional volcano
was heated up and freed.
Frozen as I was by my own alcoholic haze,
I was caught off guard until the jolt
freed me from my alcoholic daze,
not unlike victims embedded in ash
who were frozen in frigid pose
that ended their mad dash.
The only difference
is that they were never able to get free.
But if Pompei's citizens ran too late,
at least they knew enough
to run for their lives.
There you go, you say.
Once again, you've unsheathed your sword.
Even when you try to defend me,
you become besotted by criticism.
"Besotted," I answer, "would be the correct word."

Hacksaw Ridge

Is there evil in all of us that remains dormant
until ungodly forces take hold?
Clint Eastwood's film gives an answer
that is straightforward and bold.
Japanese forces control a certain ridge
(more like a high plateau or redoubt)
and the Marines are ordered
to climb up there
and force the enemy out.
Like speeding freight trains
the two sides collide head on.
Here is hand-to-hand combat
so intense that blood spatters
in numerous places.
But the real impact comes
when we study the faces--
a Japanese soldier whose expression,
distorted with wrath and hate,
mirrors that of the enraged Marine
he is trying to eviscerate.
So much for the innocent dogface,
the former deacon, acolyte or Eagle Scout.
All disappear in the frenzy of war
when the darkest part of our inner nature.
dodges all pretense and decides to come out.

Aversion to Subversion

This can't be happening to me.
At sixty-four I've got a lot of life left to see.
They told me to leave,
to get out of Germany,
or I'd end up dead,
but I didn't hear.
My Iron Cross First Class
would protect me, I said.
Now I see that the vestiges of my past valor
had gone to my head.

Here I stand naked and shaken by fear
in a long line of terrified old men
who, like me, know that death must be near.
Is mankind truly capable of such evil?
Considering what I see
surrounding me now,
the answer can only be yes.
Still, I'm convinced that God
will preserve my soul
in this time of monumental upheaval
and stress.

Most of the naked men with me in line
use their hands to cover their private parts.
Why such modesty?
Following death in the "showers" by gas
their manhood will be burned away
a short time before they toss
what's left into a series of waiting carts.

One good outcome remains.
As bad as it will be and has been,
in this hell on earth,
I'm convinced that I'm headed for Heaven
where I'll experience a dramatic rebirth.
At the end, there's no need to despair.
A second assignment to hell
just wouldn't be fair.

A Marble Index (Part Two)

A marble index,
smooth and cold,
huge in size,
a man-god,
not yet old,
naked to the world,
with slingshot in view,
an eye-opening physique,
tied to strong moral sinew,
a look so serious,
a rendering so faultless all in all
as to be mysterious.
And note the eyes—
a far-off stare
a menacing look.
Such perfection in an ancient time
is something the modern world must laud.
It gives evidence
that the sculptor's hard chisel
was directed by the hand of God.

My Favorite Poem

I'm winding down.
This book contains more than ninety poems,
each one having elicited a quantity of sweat
while slicing off a bit of my soul.
If I were a car, I'd be out of fuel.
Without help, there's a good chance
I'll begin to hyperventilate and drool.
It's high time I found another poet
to help with my finish.
At first, I go to Matthew Arnold*
whose fame never seems to diminish.
"Dover Beach" is one of my favorites:
> Ah, love, let us be true
> To one another! For the world which seems
> To lie before us like a land of dreams,
> So various, so beautiful, so new,
> Hath really neither joy, nor love, nor light,
> Nor certitude, nor peace, nor help for pain;
> And we are here as on a darkling plain
> Swept with confused alarms of struggle and flight,
> Where ignorant armies clash by night.

This last stanza describes Arnold's view of life.
As we can easily ascertain,
it is a view reflecting inner strife
inspired by observations at seaside
that have elicited an onslaught of pain:
> the grating roar/Of pebbles
> which the waves draw back and fling
> At their return, up the high strand.

For him such activity underscores:
    the turbid ebb and flow/Of human misery.

I conclude that the mood set by Arnold is much too perverse
to be included with any final bit of verse.
Instead of Arnold, I need a poem that sets a happier pace.
William Wordsworth, a famous Romantic poet,
may be the one to take his place.
In "I Wandered Lonely as a Cloud" ** the poet sees:
    a crowd/A host of golden daffodils
    Beside the lake, beneath the trees
    Fluttering and dancing in the breeze.

    They stretched in never-ending line
    Along the margin of a bay:
    Ten thousand saw I at a glance,
    Tossing their heads in sprightly dance.

The last stanza summarizes his thoughts:
    For oft when on my couch I lie
    In vacant or in pensive mood,
    They flash upon the inward eye
    Which is the bliss of solitude;
    And then my heart with pleasure fills,
    And dances with the daffodils.

Obviously, this stanza is in stark contrast
to Arnold's pessimistic rant:
Surely, this is the light mood I've been seeking.
On the other hand, Wordsworth proves he's unwilling or unable
to give his view a spiritual slant.
He fails to note that the beauty he notes
on paper and in his head
comes not from nature, but from God instead.

Soon, I conclude that Robert Browning provides a better voice in "The Year's at the Spring:" ***

>The year's at the spring,
>And day's at the morn;
>Morning's at seven;
>The hillside's dew-pearled;
>The lark's on the wing;
>The snail's on the thorn;
>God's in His Heaven—
>And all's right with the world.

* Harmon, William, ed. THE TOP FIVE HUNDRED POEMS. New York: Columbia University Press, 1992. p.706.
**Ibid, p.396.
***Ibid, p.670

My Favorite Poem (Part Two)

God's in His Heaven—
All's right with the world.
Robert Browning*
has conveyed the feeling
that has come to me today,
here in Shepherdstown
where the air is clean,
and the buds are ready
to spring forth
in a colorful array.
How do the agnostics react?
What do the atheists say?
God isn't in His Heaven
because God doesn't exist
so, stuff your good feelings
when they come.
You've got to resist.
How morose these people must be.
They ignore the evidence
the rest of us see—
the regularity of the seasons;
the immensity of the oceans;
the miracle of the human body
(particularly the brain);
earth's perfect placement
in our solar system;
replenishment following the rain;
above all, the phenomenon known as love—
just a few of the many reasons
that help some of us to conclude

that there's something out there
outside of ourselves.
If I encounter people
who are on the brink of believing,
I always give them a shove.

Ibid.

Missed Opportunity

Omaha, Utah,
words fail me as I gaze at the beaches
beneath me, now deserted,
imagining the carnage,
the cries of the wounded
riddled by clattering machineguns
hidden in enemy pill boxes,
untouched despite numerous
bombing runs.

*Gallant fliers,
how could you miss
the entrenchments,
and the menacing enemy guns.*

It was the cloud cover, they answer,
We were blinded and couldn't see.

*But the British bombers
obliterated their targets
without sending their bombs
harmlessly into the sea.*

*That's because
they flew under the clouds
while pursuing their attack,
a strategy that seemed brash
when one considers the exposure to flak.*

But you flew straight and pretty

*when you dropped incendiaries
at a safe altitude on a wooden city.*

*At the time,
there was no room for pity
as we told you many times before.
The subhuman enemy
wouldn't end the war
even after flames killed so many.*

They continued.
"War is hell," as Sherman once said.
We'll need something much bigger
that will leave many more of them dead,
plus, we'll want to teach the Russians
that if ever they decide to flex their muscles
they should pass over the U.S.
and choose some other target instead.

*You mean there are mixed motives.
Are we stalling the peace talks
until the Bomb is complete
so the world can witness the mushroom cloud
as well as the surrender of an enemy
that took so long to defeat.*

If your answer isn't **no**,
*please don't tell me.
It's not something I want to know.*

Often Bugged

Have you ever noticed
that the world doesn't love tics?
They are ugly little things
that often bring disease.
Small wonder then
that the sight of one
will often make us feel ill at ease.
I felt one on my neck the other day
and quickly flicked it
through the open car door.
From my mouth, came a sound
I don't often make—
EEAGHHHHUGGGAAAAAAAAA!!!
It's the same reaction I'd give to a rat
or a rattlesnake.
I've often considered
how disconcerting it would be,
if the world reacted in a similar fashion
when the masses confronted me.

Wait! I spoke too soon.
As a Conservative in Shepherdstown, WV
with no place to go
I've often aroused similar passion,
even from Liberals I don't know.

Oscar Reborn

Oscar, Oscar.
How far you fell.
Before you hit bottom,
no one would have disputed
that you had it made.
Then came jail time
for an offense that today
would be heralded in any
Gay Pride parade.
Your grave is near downtown Paris
in the Pere Lachaise Cemetery
where you took up residence
in November of 1900.
You chose to die then
because you hoped for
new status
in a new century,
something more than a novelty
or a forgotten aberration.
You'll be pleased to know
that you succeeded.
Your high place has been restored--
you have become a sensation
whose presence is sorely needed,
a pacesetter who is now adored.
Do you know that the caretakers
had to protect your grave
with a plastic shell
because so many visitors
wanted to kiss the stone?

Be assured that you are not forgotten
and you are certainly not alone.

No Flashback

Lunch at the club.
My father with my help
hobbles toward the door
at the far end of the patio.
Diners at various outside tables
pretend they don't hear him
cut wind and moan.
I see the two of us
leaning forward
toward the patio door
and then we both stumble
into the lower lobby,
up the stairs
(with the help of an electric lift),
and finally, down a long hall
that leads
to the men's locker room.
Is it too far to go?
Will he make it?
No, he doesn't.

Why does this memory
come to me now?
After all this time?
He is long dead,
this once virile man
who taught me to fish
and to swim
and showed me what honor was.
And then it hits me.

What I'm seeing in memory
is no flashback.
It's what I'm experiencing right now.
I'm the same doddering old man today
that he was then.

Rest assured, Old Man,
that I'm in the same rut.
You provided the template
that I must follow.
utilizing a pattern
that has already been cut.

A Near-Death Experience

I had a near-death experience
the other day
when an attendant stuffed me into
the bore of an MRI scanner
in a most undignified way.
The banging and crashing inside
relieved my claustrophobia
(but only briefly).
Mental diversions
would be needed, I concluded,
to keep me from screaming,
not like Harry Palmer's ploy
in the Ipcress File
(a nail in palm of the hand),
but mental diversions instead—
like remembering Dana's down-rush
(the first of several such rides)
through a red tube toward a soothing light,
much like a descent
through a blood vessel, she cried,
with shoulders touching the sides—
or my own brush with death
on the airport road at night.

You've only got fifteen minutes left.
the attendant says.
You lie, I think to myself.
*Your refrain was identical
a half hour ago.*

If a tunnel is an essential near-death ingredient,
as with Dana who ultimately
lost her cancer fight,
the road to hell must be looked at
in a totally different light—
no comfortable descent
no soothing light.
In fact, it has got to be quite similar
to what I experienced the other day
except they'll be no attendant
to help me keep my fears at bay.

You only have ten minutes left,
she says, trying to put me at ease.
Sure, I think to myself,
And the moon is made of Limburger cheese.

Prelate Under Glass

Come and see.
A prelate under glass.
It's quite a curiosity.
He's well preserved,
just like Lenin,
and like Lenin
his skin has taken on
a saffron-like hue
highlighted by starkly white vestments
confirming his high station
as is certainly his due.
Christianity, now dead,
is a tourist attraction
offering this shrine
to the late Bishop of Rome,
laid out in a glass case
in stark-white clothes
where he resides all alone
inside an Islamic mosque
(formerly St. Peters)
striking an eternal pose.
How could we have missed the signs?
When they said, *Kill the Infidels*
they meant, *Kill the Infidels*.
What fools we were
to have ignored such predilections,
and when the bombs came down,
their hordes followed closely behind,
proof positive of their intention
to snatch anything of ours they could find
if only to destroy it.
Meanwhile, the latest Hajj
is not to Mecca,
but to Rome.

A Father She Can Trust

On the phone from Denver
you suddenly put forth a gentle attack.
My religious commitment left me, you said,
until my new husband brought it back.
How can that be, I ask,
when our family's regular church attendance
was intended to put you on a spiritual track?
Then you use words
that every father dreads.
Your hypocrisy became apparent
when I discovered your cheating ways.
I wanted to say that *the cheating ways* occurred
before I discovered the appropriate meds.
I also wanted to point out
that bipolar sufferers
experience heightened sexual urges
until Lithium is poured like water on the flames.
I would never have described the primary reason—
her mother's disease put sex out of season.
But the words, any words, wouldn't come.
They remained stuck in my throat.
She would never believe that life in the meatgrinder
was as repellant to me as it was to her, and
that guilt feelings always have a way
of putting holes in any boat guided by passion and lust.
Will she ever believe that with the proper meds in place,
I've become a father she can trust?

Black Water

A fortune teller's warning:
Beware of black water.
Those words gripped her
from a young age,
making her deathly afraid
of water of any type,
ocean, pool or lake,
an aversion that meant
that any chance encounter with water
would be more than she could take.
How then could she become
a floating corpse at night
near Santa Catalina Island?
Imagine her fright
as she screamed for help
in the black water beside her yacht
and the fruitless efforts
to avoid a fate that would come to her
no matter how hard she fought.
The prophecy was etched in stone.
She could accept the inevitable drowning
but not the horror of drowning alone.

Toppled Egos

Complacent fishermen,
too exhausted to come up on deck
and eager to avoid the shattering cold,
remain asleep in their bunks
while seawater and mist accumulate
on the vessel's topside,
forming a crust of ice
so thick that the craft
eventually flips over and sinks.
To avoid this toppling effect,
the remedy is not complex—
constant vigilance,
punctuated by well-placed axe blows
to displace the ice.

A perfect analogy!

How many times
have we observed
ever-increasing egos
topple one historical figure
after another?
Inflated and top heavy
from a buildup of self-centeredness,
their popularity eventually flips
sending them to the bottom—
Julius Caesar at the Rubicon,
Napoleon and Hitler in Russia,
MacArthur in North Korea,
Nixon at Watergate,

McCarthy at the Army- McCarthy hearings,
and so many others.
Unfortunately,
unlike ice-threatened ships
there is no known remedy.

Memorable Neighbors

The Eynon's were in the next block.
The family lost George senior
to heart disease
and son David to hepatitis
and George junior to cancer.
Ed Chalfant expired
after diving into a frigid lake.
The Trondel's snooty daughter
told my sister to stay away.
Mrs. Dyke, our landlady,
received Dad's hand-delivered check
with style and grace.
Martha Vogt
spotted naked swimmers nearby,
married but not to each other.
Of course, we had the alcoholic
(actually, two or three alcoholics),
a nasty spinster,
one pregnant teenager,
a cheating husband,
two suicides,
a young friend lost to cancer,
a blond-haired girl,
one of my early crushes,
who suffered with me when
I forgot to bring money for the movies.
Best of all, was the annual Christmas party
(at our house in Highland Park)
when the neighbors gathered
to taste Father's special eggnog.

They would always be there
(or so I once thought).
Gone forever now,
they gather as misty figures
round my leather chair
minutes before I fall asleep.

Coco

She should have been shot.
Petain at age eighty-four
was too old to be executed
for the betrayal of the French nation,
but she was not.
A collaborator, yes,
but also a spy.
She worked for the Abwehr
and had a Nazi lover,
Baron Hans Günther von Dincklage
no less (she called him Spatz)
who recruited her into his network of spies.
An Adonis with blond-hair
and dazzling blue eyes,
he seduced her in Paris
during the Nazi occupation.
He offered her a room at the Ritz
and a Nazi chauffeur,
a show of opulence
that proved her high station.
An avid anti-Semite,
she nonetheless partnered with a Jew
who "stole" most of the revenue
from a perfume
much favored by the French.
But even a vat of Chanel No. 5
couldn't hide the stench
tied to her reputation
at the end of the war.
Her escapades made her, some said,

little more than a whore,
but her head was never shaved
and no firing squad appeared.
She got off Scot-free
after relying on deception and lies
to avoid the punishment she most feared.
Her extensive connections
responded on cue to her cries.
Winston, a longtime friend
who admired her cunning,
saved her from prosecution in the end.
Coco Chanel stands out as an example
of what money and power can do.
She died fabulously rich,
still addicted to morphine
while chain-smoking Camels
and thumbing her nose at all the conventions
thereby securing a place in history
as a first-class bitch.
Others would disagree
arguing that she was a brilliant couturier
whose fashions set the pace,
but her late comeback
was scorned by the French fashion elite
who gloated when she fell on her face.
Memory of her past Nazi collaboration
probably made them somewhat callous.
Still, her stylish suits and the little black dress
were highly popular despite the underlying malice.
Can we ever forget Chanel's pink ensemble
(covered with blood) that Jackie wore
on that fatal day in Dallas?

Reparations

Reparations for slavery?
It's too far back
Tracking is impossible.
It's another empty round
in the Far Left's overstretched attack.
If any race deserves reparations,
it's the Jews.
Six million murdered.
Have you ever seen the shoes
piled high as mountains,
and the hair stuffed into bushels?
Save bullets, Himmler said.
Shoot the mother through the infant,
using one round instead of two.
German efficiency!
So that we don't lose count,
the Germans should pay
for every lost Jew.
Yes, they were Nazis, but they were Germans first.
Have you seen the newsreels of Hitler?
The adoration and the praise
The exuberant faces about to burst.
It was a national tragedy.
Every German from that generation forward
is part of a cadre that should be cursed.

What's that?
You say I'm biased in my views.
Yes, I admit I've used ancestry.com.
I also admit that the testing determined

that 4% of my genetic lineage belongs to the Jews.
Even so, I find your assessment somewhat amusing
since the remaining heritage is split between English and German.
Therefore, my supposed bias is present or absent
depending on which result you're using.

Acknowledgements

My wife Shannon gave me encouragement and support from the beginning. She was even able to put up with my long disappearances as I sat alone in my office composing in front of my computer. When editing was necessary (and it always was), she offered her assistance without regret.

Kendra Adkins Goldsborough, the owner of Four Seasons Bookstore in Shepherdstown, was also very supportive. She provided shelf space and display areas which contributed greatly to the enthusiastic response by local poetry lovers. When the time was right, she offered space on the second floor for my readings.

About the Author

Never Alone in a Cemetery was the first book of poetry that Rick published. Then followed *Headstone in the Headlights*. Rick jokes that the current book, *Musings Under a Buckboard,* has gotten him out of the graveyard at last. He is a graduate of Pitt Law School and Denison University who presently resides in Shepherdstown, West Virginia (near the battlefield of Antietam). His poetry has been featured in Eureka and in the California Quarterly. "A Time to Walk the Ocean Floor" and "As Large as the Universe" appeared in Volume 25, Number 2 (2006) of Westview, a publication of Southwestern Oklahoma State University. In November of 2005 "Foxfire" was awarded third place in the 2005 Pennwriters Poetry Contest. On January 2, 2010, his poem entitled "Never Alone in the Cemetery" appeared in the Pittsburgh Post-Gazette. Several of his poems were recently published in Good News, a local newspaper. *Never Alone in a Cemetery* was first on the 2018 fiction best seller list tallied by Four Seasons Bookstore in Shepherdstown. Copies of all three books can be purchased at any local bookstore or through Amazon.

www.ingramcontent.com/pod-product-compliance
Lightning Source LLC
Chambersburg PA
CBHW071409290426
44108CB00014B/1743